The World of
Jane Austen

BRENDA WILLIAMS

A Lady of Letters

Jane Austen lived during years of enormous change, the time of the American, French and Industrial Revolutions. There was a population boom: 'Too many children,' she commented, having experienced the deaths of two sisters-in-law at their eleventh confinements. Agriculture was still the basis of the economy: her clergyman father was also a farmer and her brother owned a country estate. Canals carried trade goods; coaches carried people and post. A European war raged and great British victories were won at Trafalgar and Waterloo. Fortunes were to be made in India and the Caribbean but the slave trade was under fierce attack. Jane, intelligent and educated, knew all about the issues of her day and her life was touched by many of them, yet her writing considers them only in relation to her own burning interest: human nature and human society. In their portrayal she has few equals, but it is the society of Georgian England in which her characters play out their lives that is the world of Jane Austen.

LEFT *Jane Austen, sketched by her sister Cassandra c. 1810.*

BELOW *A novel setting: this 18th-century hilltop mansion overlooking a peaceful village provides a glimpse into the world of Jane Austen.*

The Village

Jane Austen was born on a bitter winter's night, 16 December 1775, in a Hampshire country parsonage. The seventh child of the Reverend George Austen, rector of Steventon, and his wife Cassandra, she was their second daughter. 'She is to be Jenny,' wrote her father, who christened her more formally, as Jane, after her mother's sister.

The baptism was performed in the small stone church of St Nicholas, next to the squire's manor house where the Digweed family lived. Steventon was a small village. Its single row of cottages, some way from the rectory, housed around 30 families but had neither inn nor shop. The parsonage was roomy, in contrast to the village homes. It had seven bedrooms and three attics, allowing the Austens to set up a school for boys.

The family already comprised James, George, Edward, Henry, Cassandra (named after her mother) and Francis. After Jane came another baby, Charles. Supporting this growing family proved challenging on a clergyman's income. Despite receiving some £210 a year from the parishes of Steventon and Deane, plus income from his school and farm, Jane's father had sometimes to borrow from richer relatives.

A scholar at Tonbridge School, Kent, and St John's College, Oxford, George Austen was ordained at Rochester Cathedral before returning to teach at Tonbridge. He then went back to Oxford and, while staying in Bath, met Cassandra Leigh, niece of the Master of Balliol College. The couple married at St Swithin, Walcot, Bath, in 1764, with

ABOVE *Steventon Rectory, Jane Austen's childhood home, drawn by her niece Anna. Mr Austen's pupils slept in the topmost rooms.*

OPPOSITE, CLOCKWISE FROM FAR LEFT

St Nicholas's church at Steventon in Hampshire filled Jane Austen's childhood memories. Here she was christened and heard her father, who was rector for over 30 years, preach on Sundays.

Jane Austen's mother, Cassandra Leigh, married George Austen in 1764. Mrs Austen was proud of her family, and its ownership of Stoneleigh Abbey in Warwickshire.

A portrait of the young George Austen, whose Kentish family had been in the wool trade for generations. Considered good-looking, as was his wife, the 'handsome rector' was an affectionate father to his eight children.

Cassandra dressed in a dashing red riding habit that she wore home to Hampshire. George Austen was 32; his new wife 24.

Mrs Austen helped with the school, feeding, clothing and nursing her own children as well as the schoolboys. To keep the parsonage running smoothly, she sent each child to live with a village family when they were a few months old. A country wet nurse could ask two shillings and sixpence a week for her services, although the young Austens were probably weaned before leaving their mother. The parents paid daily visits, according to a grandson, and took the toddlers home for family occasions. The children returned home permanently when less dependent. This rearing system seemed to be successful. In an age of high infant mortality, before the introduction of inoculation, all the young Austens survived, including George, who was handicapped and needed special care all his life.

Jane's early days were therefore spent in a tiny country cottage, eating, sleeping and playing with the village children. Learning to walk, tumble and talk with them, she acquired in the process a local Hampshire accent.

BELOW *This romantic view of 18th-century life is shown in* Applepickers by a Cottage in a Wooded Landscape with Chichester Beyond *by George Smith (1714–76).*

The Church and Clergy

In the 18th century the country parson was central to village life. He might, like Mr Austen, set up a school, helped by his wife and daughters, who also visited the poor and sick, taking them nourishment and warm clothing. The Church was often chosen as a career by younger sons of the landed gentry, hoping to be granted parishes on a family estate, such as in *Mansfield Park*. Promotion, as in other careers, often needed the support of a patron. George Austen owed his living at Steventon, and the right to run Cheesedown Farm, to its absentee landlord, Thomas Knight, husband of a second cousin. Some country squires themselves became parsons. The less scrupulous of these 'squarsons' left parish duties to a poorly paid curate while living the high life of a sporting squire or 'hunting parson'. Local parishes might also be handed down through the generations.

ABOVE *Mr Collins, the clergyman cousin, declares himself to Elizabeth Bennet, an illustration by Hugh Thompson (1860–1920) for* Pride and Prejudice.

LEFT *Mrs Anne Lefroy, Jane's neighbour at Ashe Rectory, encouraged Jane's literary interests.*

James Austen held Steventon after his father retired. He also enjoyed hunting.

Jane Austen's family was close and well-connected. She had a widespread web of cousins, many of them clergymen, throughout the southern counties of England. It is not surprising that her attitudes to churchmen are sharply observed in her novels. She censures Dr Grant's selfish gluttony in *Mansfield Park*; holds to ridicule the obsequious Mr Collins of *Pride and Prejudice*, in total thrall to his aristocratic patroness; and deplores the snobbery of Mr Elton and his wife in *Emma*. Edmund Bertram's rejection of Mary Crawford's temptations is rewarded with

Fanny Price and a handsome living in *Mansfield Park*, while conscientious Edward Ferrars in *Sense and Sensibility* is honoured for preferring a country living to a glittering career.

Many of Jane Austen's friends were also connected to church families. One of the closest was Martha Lloyd, who later shared a home with Mrs Austen, Cassandra and Jane. Mrs Lloyd was a clergyman's widow who, in the spring of 1789, arrived in the locality with her daughters Mary and Martha. They were cousins of a family called Fowle, whose boys had been to the Austen school. Mrs Lloyd rented Deane parsonage from Mr Austen.

Near Deane was the village of Ashe, where the Reverend George Lefroy had lived in the rectory with his wife Anne and three children since 1783. Mrs, or Madam, Lefroy was quick-witted, elegant and willing to spare time to discuss prose and poetry with the young Jane. She soon became a close confidante and mentor, giving advice and encouragement in the matter of reading, perhaps discussing the essays of Dr Johnson that Jane had discovered in *The Rambler* magazine. Dr Johnson and the poet William Cowper became her favourite 'moral' writers.

ABOVE *St John's College, Oxford, drawn by Michael Rooker (1743–1801).*

BELOW Hunting Scene, *by Richard Barrett Davis (1782–1854), from The Vyne at Sherborne St John, Hampshire.*

To School

The young Austens learned their first letters and numbers, as was usual, from their mother, who entertained them with the witty verses she composed. They also had access to their father's library of 500 books, his microscope and globe. The boys in his schoolroom received Mr Austen's scholarly instruction in Latin, Greek and mathematics, although some needed encouragement, like the pupil reminded by one of Mrs Austen's verses to return after the Christmas holidays. Pupils slept in the attics and did their homework in the parlour. When ready, they left for their next schools, Eton or Winchester.

The Austens' was one of many small schools catering for the middle and upper classes, although other children remained at home, learning from tutors or governesses. Jane Austen had no high opinion of schoolteachers, possibly through experience: 'I would rather be a teacher at a school (and I can think of nothing worse) than marry a man I did not like ... I would rather do anything than be a teacher at a school,' may express her own views. At the age of seven she went with Cassandra and their cousin Jane Cooper to a school in Oxford run by Jane Cooper's aunt, widow of a Master of Brasenose College. Jane had

RIGHT *James Austen, eldest of Jane's six brothers, and a clergyman. The Austens remained a closely knit family, and towards the end of her life Jane was especially fond of James's son, Edward.*

BELOW *A village school. A mixed class of various ages shares a small schoolroom and a single teacher.*

ABOVE *The Abbey School, Reading, to which Jane and Cassandra were sent in 1784.*

LEFT *Brasenose College and the Radcliffe Library, engraved by J. Bluck (fl. 1791–1831), after an aquatint by A.C. Pugin (1762–1832). From* A History of Oxford *published in 1814.*

refused to be parted from her sister. Older brother James, studying at St John's College, was probably expected to keep an eye on the girls.

Running a school or becoming a governess, like Jane Fairfax in *Emma,* was one of the few means by which respectable women could earn a living, but schools varied in quality. Some served poor food, or not enough, taught little, but set hours of tasks such as sewing, and provided cold rooms and shared beds. Women who barely existed on the fees they could charge were always looking to save pennies, so breakfast might be hot water with a dash of milk and a roll. A typical curriculum for girls would include dancing, handwriting, French, Italian, the Bible, arithmetic, history and geography.

More dangerous than discomfort or privation was illness, as common ailments could spread like wildfire in shared accommodation. When Jane, Cassandra and their cousin all fell ill with fever in the summer of 1783, Jane Cooper disobeyed instructions not to inform parents, and probably saved Jane's life. Mrs Austen dashed to the school, which had moved to Southampton, and nursed her daughters back to health. Jane Cooper's mother caught the infection and died.

The girls returned home. Jane, aged eight, could now read any book in English and some in French, and a year she later attended the Abbey School in Reading run by Madame La Tournelle (the professional name of Sarah Hackitt). In her sixties

and sporting a cork leg, Madame La Tournelle enthralled her charges with stories of the theatre and actors. She served bread and butter breakfasts by the fire, at which young teachers might appear with hair still in curl papers. Girls slept six to a room and had morning lessons only, learning needlework, spelling and French – but Mr Austen may not have thought this education worth £35 a year. His daughters left in 1786, and Jane's schooldays came to an end.

ABOVE *A box of alphabet letters for schoolroom use, displayed at the Jane Austen's House Museum at Chawton in Hampshire.*

Home and Farm

Steventon rectory bustled with life. The household was supervised by Mrs Austen, who ensured that bread was baked, beer brewed and butter churned, that eggs were collected and honey gathered. An establishment that was home, school, farm and vicarage needed an efficient housekeeper, and Mrs Austen took charge of the dairy, vegetable garden and poultry yard. The rectory servants included maids and a cook, while once a month a washerwoman arrived to help tackle the mound of laundry produced by family and schoolboys.

Mr Austen was a practical farmer who spent time planning tasks for the agricultural year and surveying his land, crops and animals. He also took a keen interest in matters such as inter-county ploughing matches. Riding around his land on horseback, he conferred with John Bond, the farm bailiff. What would this year's crop of wheat and barley fetch? How was the market for beef and pigs? Would the weather ensure a good harvest? *Emma*'s Mr Knightley took a close interest in his estates in much the same way.

On Sundays Mr Austen donned clerical vestments to preach from the pulpit. A learned, wise, good-tempered and kindly man, he wrote his own sermons, and valued his close and happy family life. He created a pleasant atmosphere in the schoolroom, and many of his pupils became family friends. No doubt he also provided thoughtful advice and practical help to his parishioners. Jane certainly did her dutiful share of charitable giving, as her jotted accounts show.

BELOW The Reapers, 1783, an oil painting by George Stubbs (1724–1806) at Upton House in Warwickshire. The landowner rides out to see his harvesters at work, just as Mr Austen supervised the tasks on his farm.

ABOVE *A shooting party: an early 19th-century painting shows gentlemen out with their guns. Field sports were part of everyday life on an estate or farm, to provide meat for the table, control vermin and supply a pleasurable day's exercise in the fresh air.*

ABOVE *A dairymaid churns milk into butter, from* The Costume of Great Britain *engraved by William Henry Pyne. Such tasks would have been familiar to every member of the Austen family.*

BELOW *This lace collar can be seen in Jane Austen's House Museum at Chawton.*

The Austen boys and girls were expected to help when at home, and the boys remained at home until they were 12. Summer meant haymaking, when the yellowing stalks of meadow grass were raked into bundles for stacking in the June sunshine. Later, in August, came the harvesting of ripened grain. Meanwhile, the bees in the garden hives were busy producing honey, while fruit on the trees and bushes grew full and fat, ready for making jams, jellies, preserves and wine. In the autumn came the shooting and hunting season, sports taken up enthusiastically by the Austen boys. Jane's novels portray such country sports, as well as fishing, as the pursuits of gentlemen who would disappear from the house all day in enjoyment of their leisure.

Left at home, the ladies would embroider, make clothes, trim hats, practise their instruments and read. Cassandra loved to draw and Jane played the piano, as do her heroines, who are all accomplished young ladies. They might be required to play for songs and dancing, like Anne Elliot and the Bennet girls. Jane had a visiting piano teacher, an assistant organist at Winchester Cathedral called George Chard. She loved both playing and dancing, and it remained a lifelong habit with her to practise the piano daily before breakfast.

At other spare moments she might be found with pen and scrap of paper, for by the age of 12 she had begun to write stories and plays for her own and her family's amusement.

ABOVE *Jane Austen's music book shows her neatly precise notation. Greatly fond of the piano and singing, she practised daily and was remembered as having a very sweet voice by her niece Caroline. Musical skill was a desirable accomplishment for the well-bred young lady – and, therefore, Jane's heroines.*

Country Living

Mr Austen's pupils included sons of neighbouring squires and scions of the nobility, from baronets to the Earl of Portsmouth. The boys enjoyed boisterous games with the Austen children and Jane, like Catherine Morland in *Northanger Abbey*, had a grassy slope to roll down outside her home. She may also, like Catherine, have preferred cricket and rounders to dolls or pets.

Although the Austens had lived as babies with the villagers, a social gulf persisted. Village children were rarely schooled, but usually followed the occupation of their parents. Mostly the men worked on farms for around seven shillings a week, while women did spinning at home as a cottage industry, before the Industrial Revolution absorbed such work into textile factories and mills.

Some villagers found jobs in the local manor houses or rectories, as stable hands, gardeners or domestic servants. Girls became kitchenmaids, housemaids, nursemaids or dairymaids, or rose to be a lady's maid. To Jane Austen a housemaid was a 'scrub' and a kitchenmaid an 'under'. A good housekeeper's post was the pinnacle of ambition. Where would Mrs Bennet be without her Hill, or Pemberley without the housekeeper to show Mr Darcy's portrait to Elizabeth Bennet?

ABOVE *Deane House, near Steventon, where Jane visited the Harwoods. Four miles east was Manydown House, where her friends the Bigg sisters lived and where Harris Bigg-Wither proposed to Jane in 1802.*

BELOW *The Vyne, country house of the Chute family, as pictured in the magazine* Ackermann's Repository of Arts *in 1826 by John Gendall (1790–1865).*

ABOVE *Goodnestone Park in Kent, home before her marriage of Jane's sister-in-law Elizabeth Knight, the daughter of Sir Brook and Lady Bridges.*

BELOW *A lady's maid soaps her mistress's linen; oil painting by Henry Robert Morland (1730–97).*

ABOVE *Godmersham Park in Kent was the seat of Thomas Knight. Jane and her family paid extended visits to the estate on its inheritance by her brother Edward, whom the Knights adopted. This engraving of 1785 is from a painting by William Watts (1752–1851).*

The best jobs near Steventon were in the Portal paper mills which printed the Bank of England's banknotes. Here men could earn 22 shillings a week and women seven pence a day. Old age threatened poverty, however, and the Austens' bailiff, John Bond, who lost his cottage in a house fire, was saved from the workhouse by Jane's brother, James Austen, when he took the Bonds into his own home.

Although not themselves wealthy, the Austens moved in the social circles of those who were, and Mrs Austen, listing the Duke of Chandos among her antecedents, took pride in her aristocratic profile. The family joined in the round of social events and balls at such houses as The Vyne, a grand Tudor building outside Basingstoke, near James Austen's vicarage at Sherborne St John. James hunted and dined with the Chute family who lived at The Vyne and provided Members of Parliament for Hampshire. Tom Chute, 'full of wit and fun', was a favourite dance and card partner of Jane's. The Chutes were also friends of the Lefroys and of the Bigg family of Manydown House, near Deane.

There were more family connections in Kent. Great-uncle Francis Austen lived at the Red House in Sevenoaks, which Jane and Cassandra visited in 1788, and Godmersham Park was the country seat of Thomas Knight, Mr Austen's landlord. Jane and Cassandra visited there many times, attending functions at the Jacobean Chilham Castle, built in 1616. Jane mentions a famous ball held there in 1801. The Knights had taken a fancy to Jane's brother Edward, inviting him on their honeymoon in 1779, and adopted him in 1783. Edward eventually inherited Godmersham from them, having in 1791 married Elizabeth, daughter of Sir Brook and Lady Bridges of Goodnestone Park in Kent, another estate on the Austens' visiting list. By this time, Jane had taken a further step on her literary journey, completing her juvenile story, *Love and Freindship*, the year before Edward's marriage.

Estate and Landscape

The 18th-century gentleman ran a country estate. He is a character in all the Austen novels, and his attitude to the land and its workforce determined the author's perception of his moral worth. In *Persuasion*, vain Sir Walter Elliot, whose first care is for title and birth, is forced to let his estate to Admiral Croft, whose bluff bravery has won the right to his portion of English land.

Jane's brother Edward inherited his estate through chance, and was thereafter able to enhance the well-being of all his family. Not only had he Godmersham in Kent, but also extensive Hampshire properties, including Steventon Manor, let to the Digweeds, and Chawton manor house near Alton. Edward was kind and straightforward, the family businessman.

Mrs Austen had other grand relations, including cousin Thomas Leigh in his rectory at Adlestrop, Gloucestershire, and his nephew at the big house nearby, the grounds of which had been 'improved'

by the famous landscaper Humphry Repton. Successor in garden design to Lancelot 'Capability' Brown and partner of the architect John Nash, Repton's changes at Adlestrop involved enclosure of the village green, which cost villagers their access to free grazing. Such aspects of landscape design, and their desirability or otherwise, are explored in *Mansfield Park*, where Henry Crawford urges Mr Rushworth to 'modernise' at great expense, in order to show off his forefathers' house and land to better advantage.

Thomas Leigh was also heir to a property both ancient and modern. Stoneleigh Abbey in Warwickshire was a mansion completed in 1726 around the remains of a Cistercian abbey, with an Elizabethan wing and a 14th-century monastery gatehouse. Mrs Austen visited both Adlestrop and Stoneleigh with her daughters in 1806. Revelling in its grandeur, she counted the 45 windows, admired the rooms, views, grounds, servants, billiard room and variety of food, and described

BELOW *Birmingham was one of Britain's new production powerhouses, as the Industrial Revolution accelerated during Jane Austen's lifetime. A watercolour by David Cox (1783–1859) shows a landscape altered by manufacturing.*

LEFT *Antony House in Cornwall, about 1812, 'improved' by the master-landscaper Humphry Repton (1752–1818). This panoramic 'after' view is from one of the Red Books of designs produced for Repton's projects, which are discussed in* Mansfield Park.

RIGHT The Great House and Park at Chawton, c. *1780, a watercolour by Adam Callander (fl. 1780–1811).*

BELOW *Adlestrop in Gloucestershire was on the itinerary of visits made by Mrs Austen and her daughters in 1806. Cousin Thomas Leigh lived at the rectory, and his nephew at the big house. The guests were shown the expensive changes recently made to the estate by Humphry Repton.*

them in the sort of eager detail that recalls Aunt Norris's account of her visit to Mr Rushworth's Sotherton in *Mansfield Park*.

Another relative visiting Stoneleigh was the elderly Lady Saye and Sele, whom Mrs Austen reported as, 'Rather tormenting, tho' something amusing, and affords Jane many a good laugh.' In *Pride and Prejudice*, Mr Bennet observes, 'For what do we live, but to make sport for our neighbours, and laugh at them in our turn?' Yet the author, through Mr Bennet's daughter Elizabeth, counters, 'I hope I never ridicule what is wise or good. Follies and nonsense, whims and inconsistencies *do* divert me, I own, and I laugh at them whenever I can.' From Warwickshire, the Austen ladies moved to cousin Edward Cooper's family in Staffordshire, where Jane caught whooping cough.

Humphry Repton was later to make plans for the landscaping of Stoneleigh Abbey, but not many miles away a new landscape was developing in Birmingham, where James Watt and Matthew Boulton had joined forces in the year of Jane Austen's birth to develop a steam engine for industry. Mrs Elton, not always the soundest judge, declared in *Emma*, 'One has no great hopes from Birmingham.' Yet the advances of the Industrial Revolution were to transform the landscape and society of England to an unimagined degree.

At Play

The Austen family was never at a loss for amusement. At Christmas they played traditional games such as Hunt the Slipper, Oranges and Lemons, Wind the Jack, Spare Old Noll and Lighting a Candle in Haste. Dancing was always popular, at home, in friends' houses and at public balls. Jane joined energetically and tirelessly in the country dances, like Gathering Peascods, which everyone knew, and in which couples formed a circle, or a set down which they had to progress. 'There were 20 dances and I danced them all, without any fatigue,' Jane wrote to Cassandra proudly. 'I fancy I could just as well dance for a week together as for half an hour.' The Austens danced with the Lefroys, the Digweeds, the Terry family at Dummer and the Biggs at Manydown, an obliging mother or aunt sitting at the keyboard or a servant playing on the fiddle.

By the age of 17 Jane was attending the balls held at Basingstoke Assembly Rooms above the town hall. There were strict rules of etiquette, broadly based on the *Rules to be Observ'd in Bath* drawn up by Richard 'Beau' Nash in 1706. These strictures included: 'Every Lady who does not go down the set, except prevented by indisposition, precludes herself from dancing during the evening' and 'Gentlemen, Officers on duty excepted, are not admissible in boots'. To slight someone needing a partner (as did Mr Darcy) or leave a dance before its finish was considered highly impolite.

Acting was another family pastime, fascinating to Jane since the early theatricals of her childhood. During Christmas 1782, her teenage brothers presented for family and friends a tragedy set at the time of William the Conqueror. Next year saw a production in the barn of Sheridan's *The Rivals*. Further stagings were more ambitious, with painted scenery, like that introduced in the theatricals of *Mansfield Park* which so upset Fanny Price and Sir Thomas Bertram. James Austen, seen as the family writer, took theatricals seriously, providing prologues and epilogues in verse. Family friends provided actors as well as audience. One, Tom Fowle, was to become Cassandra's fiancé.

BELOW *A ball in 1815 at the fashionable Almack's Assembly Rooms in St James's, London. To the left, Beau Brummell, arbiter of London fashion, talks to the Duchess of Rutland.*

BELOW *A page from one of Jane Austen's music books.*

Mrs Jordan (mother of 10 of the Duke of Clarence's children) in *The Devil to Pay*, a farce she found highly amusing.

Reading was a treasured pastime and Jane Austen had firm favourites, beginning with Samuel Richardson's *Sir Charles Grandison*. She also read Fielding's *Tom Jones*, knew Sterne's *Tristram Shandy* and *A Sentimental Journey*, and admired Fanny Burney, Scott, Cowper and Crabbe, a favourite poet. Her story called *Elinor and Marianne*, read first to her family in 1795 (and later re-titled *Sense and Sensibility*), took its initial form in the letter-written narrative of Richardson's novels.

ABOVE *The famous actress Mrs Jordan (1762–1816) amused the Austen family at Covent Garden. She became a neighbour of Henry Austen's in London when the Duke of Clarence rejected her in 1811.*

RIGHT *A 1780 illustration from* Tom Jones, *by Henry Fielding, one of Jane Austen's favourite novels.*

BELOW *Dance Lesson, a painting by Niclas Lafrensen (1737–1807). Dancing masters were in demand to teach fashionable ladies and gentlemen the skills of the ballroom.*

Family theatricals remained a popular Austen amusement and Jane was soon writing plays of her own. The family made careful choices when performing, from dramas by Hannah Cowley and Susannah Centlivre among others. As an adult, Jane enjoyed many theatre outings in the provinces and in London, where in 1813 she was at Covent Garden to see the famous actress

A Widening World

Steventon and its parsonage were not immune from radical changes in the wider world. Mr Austen's sister Philadelphia had sailed to India alone at the age of 21 to find her fortune, and there she married a Mr Hancock who did business with Warren Hastings, the future Governor of India. Hastings, whose wife was dead, may have fathered Philadelphia's child, Elizabeth. His own young son was sent to school in 1764, in the care of the newly married Austens, but tragically died.

Aunt Philadelphia and her daughter, known as Eliza, brought a touch of the exotic to the Austens' world. Cousin Eliza, 14 when Jane was born, was sophisticated, lively, spoke French, kept a horse in London, went to Almack's Assembly Rooms, called on duchesses, was at a ball with Queen Marie-Antoinette and had jewels sent from India. In 1781 she married a Frenchman who later died on the guillotine in the French Revolution. The uprising had begun in 1789, a year after Warren Hastings stood trial for corruption in London, watched by Eliza and her mother.

ABOVE *A portrait of William Wilberforce (1759–1833), founder of the Society for the Abolition of the Slave Trade. The 1794 painting is by Anton Hickel (1745–98). Jane Austen refers to the issue of slavery in* Mansfield Park.

ABOVE *William Pitt the Younger speaking in the House of Commons, 1793. Prime Minister at the age of 24, Pitt led Britain during the long war with revolutionary and imperial France.*

At this time Jane, whose life had begun at the time of the American War of Independence, was working on *Lady Susan*. George III had suffered his first fit of madness, Pitt was Prime Minister and radical ideas were in the air. Such items of front-page news make little stir in the Austen novels: it is their effects on everyday life and ideas that are presented. Abolition of the slave trade, urged by William Wilberforce, was a subject on which the Austen views were made clear in *Mansfield Park*, where the topic appears explicitly and also hovers implicitly over the precise position of Fanny in the Bertram household. The book was written in 1812–13, some six years after slave-trading by British ships had been outlawed by Parliament following Wilberforce's campaign, but slavery remained an issue arousing strong feelings and vigorous

debate. The war with Napoleon's France echoes throughout *Persuasion* and was felt close to home. Cassandra's fiancé Tom Fowle sailed as an army chaplain in 1795 with troops fighting the French in the West Indies. He had been promised a living in Shropshire on his return, sufficient to support a wife, but Tom died of fever off San Domingo in 1797 and Cassandra remained single, despite the beauty that attracted other suitors. Instead it was her brother Henry who was married that year, to his widowed cousin Eliza.

The Napoleonic Wars touched the Austen family closely, the brothers playing their part, and wherever in the world the action took them, letters from sister Jane brought news of home and family, while she in return received first-hand tales of their adventures.

Other news to shake the Austen world included the rumbling of the Industrial Revolution with the Luddite riots, the assassination of Prime Minister Spencer Perceval in 1812, and the escapades of the scandalous Lord Byron. Britain was changing:

Jane was seven when James Watt demonstrated his improved factory steam engine, and in 1814 George Stephenson built his first railway locomotive, pioneering a technology that would soon transform the country.

ABOVE *Luddites rampage: textile workers protest against mechanical looms threatening the home craft of hand-weaving.*

Seaside and Outings

The Austen family spent a good deal of time visiting each other. Jane and Cassandra were often in demand by their brothers and sisters-in-law for confinements and child care. They visited brother Henry in London and brother Edward in Kent, where social gatherings in grand houses such as Godmersham and Goodnestone found their way into *Pride and Prejudice* which, as *First Impressions,* took form in 1796.

Seaside holidays were growing fashionable, as sea-bathing was promoted for health, rivalling the established spas. The Prince Regent led the way when he created the resort of Brighton, transforming the modest Sussex farmhouse he shared with Mrs Fitzherbert into the outlandishly exotic Royal Pavilion. Such attractions were not to all tastes, however: 'I assure you that I dread the idea of going to Brighton,' wrote Jane to Cassandra in 1799, unlike her creation Lydia Bennet, who longs for the round of frivolity promised by the seaside, together with a camp full of soldiers.

Jane took holidays with her parents to Devon: Sidmouth in 1801, and Dawlish and Teignmouth the following year. Mr Austen, an

LEFT *Brighton in Sussex, showing the Old Pavilion and Steyne, engraved by Charles Richards. The Prince Regent, later George IV, rides before onlookers drawn to the newly fashionable seaside resort. Jane Austen was not among the Regent's admirers.*

RIGHT *Sidmouth in Devon, pictured in 1797. The Austens spent a summer holiday here in 1801, when sea dips were made from a bathing machine like those seen on the beach.*

BELOW *Dovedale in the Peak District, by Joseph Wright of Derby (1734–97). The attractions of the area in* Pride and Prejudice *included Mr Darcy's Pemberley.*

ABOVE A View of Box Hill, Surrey, with Dorking in the Distance, *painted in 1733 by George Lambert (1700–65). The scene had not greatly changed when Jane described a visit to the popular beauty spot in* Emma.

enthusiastic tourist, may also have taken his wife and daughters to Tenby and Barmouth in Wales in 1802. They chose a November break at Lyme Regis in Dorset in 1803 and again in 1804. Here Jane took pleasure in cliff-top walks with Henry. Cassandra later accompanied Henry and his wife Eliza to the smarter Weymouth, just along the coast. Left to herself, Jane walked on the Cobb and attended the Lyme Assembly Rooms, where two violins and a cello played for Tuesday dancing. Mrs Austen played cards. During one of these trips, Jane is said to have had a brief romantic episode with a young man who made plans to visit the family, but died.

ABOVE The Harbour and the Cobb, Lyme Regis, by Moonlight, *a painting by Copplestone Warre Bamfylde (1717–91). This picture shows the scene of Louisa Musgrove's fall in* Persuasion. *Jane visited Lyme in November 1803.*

After Mr Austen's death, a family stay in Worthing, Sussex, was planned by Edward for September 1805, despite the renewed threat of invasion from France. Fanny Knight records Aunt Jane winning 18 shillings in a raffle one evening, after a day in which she herself had bought fish on the beach with her grandmother, and taken a sea dip with her mother and governess. This was a prolonged visit for Jane, Cassandra, Martha Lloyd and Mrs Austen, possibly lasting over Christmas. Jane loved the exhilaration of sea-bathing, even in November, a donkey-drawn bathing machine carrying her down to the water, with an attendant maid.

The novels include famous outings: to Lyme in *Persuasion*, Box Hill in *Emma*, Mr Rushworth's Sotherton in *Mansfield Park*, the Peak District and Pemberley in *Pride and Prejudice*. A change of scene invigorates the plot or provides a dramatic backdrop for events such as Louisa Musgrove's fall on the Lyme Regis Cobb in *Persuasion*. These scenes were drawn from their author's first-hand experience, or from her reading.

Her last, unfinished, novel, *Sanditon*, written in 1817, incorporates the creation of a seaside resort (hence the title), possibly Bognor in Sussex. To it, Mr Parker, an entrepreneur, hopes to attract visitors repelled by the vulgarities of Brighton.

Fashion

Jane loved to shop, though she seems to have had little care for her appearance, cropping her brunette curls short around her face, and roughly pinning up her back hair or tucking it under a cap. Cassandra was a beauty; Jane was acknowledged as pretty, with doll-like, highly coloured cheeks, small nose and mouth, and sparkling, intelligent eyes ('fine eyes', like Elizabeth Bennet's). Tom Fowle's impression was of 'quite a child, very lively and full of humour'. She was tall, slim, upright, elegant, light of foot, lively and healthy-looking but, fine though her individual features were, radiating character, she failed to achieve the description of 'handsome'.

Jane was content to have her hair dressed by Nanny Littlewart from the village and, when submitted to a hair restyling in London in 1813, disliked the result. 'My hair was at least tidy, which was all my ambition,' she claimed after a ball. Too great an interest in clothes and appearance is given short shrift in the novels, where vanity all too often means vacuity.

Nevertheless, the Austen sisters spent many hours in making, altering and repairing their clothes. They learned sewing from Mrs Austen, who transformed her red wedding outfit, for example, into a riding jacket for young Francis.

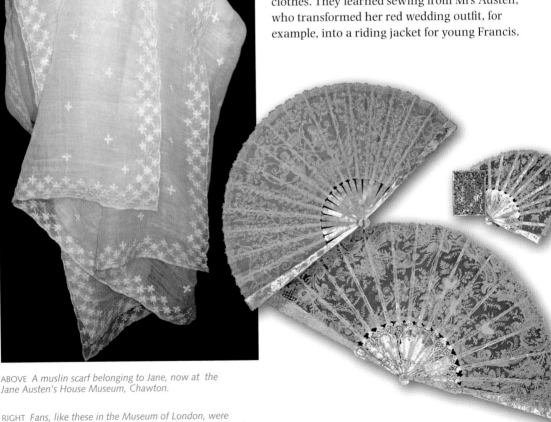

ABOVE *A muslin scarf belonging to Jane, now at the Jane Austen's House Museum, Chawton.*

RIGHT *Fans, like these in the Museum of London, were carried by ladies to cool themselves in stuffy, crowded and candle-lit assembly rooms, and for whispering behind.*

ABOVE *Evening dresses for the summer of 1808, as illustrated in* Le Beau Monde, *or* Literary and Fashionable Magazine.

ABOVE *Two young ladies in calico gowns ride in a phaeton: from Humphry Repton's* Gallery of Fashion.

Nor was fashion neglected. Out of a yearly budget of some £50, Jane spent £14 on clothes in 1807 and £8 on laundry. She bought silk stockings at 12 shillings a pair in London, and purchased four pairs of stockings and six shifts from a pedlar at Steventon.

Jane and Cassandra were quick to adopt caps, worn at home by middle-aged women: Jane took to hers by the age of 23. She enjoyed more glamorous headgear sometimes, borrowing a Marmalouc cap – in vogue after Nelson's victory at the Nile in 1798 – for a grand ball at Kempshott Park. Increased trade with India led to the wider availability of new materials, and revolutionary unrest in France caused French dressmakers to set up in London, so books and newspapers were full of fashion news and illustrations. In *Pride and Prejudice* Mrs Gardiner brings news of the latest London fashions to the Bennet household and

Jane's letters detailed keen observation of what was in style. Hats, muffs, parasols and reticules were desired accessories. Straw hats were for morning wear and Mrs Lefroy, a woman of 'genius, taste and tenderness of soul', according to Jane, set up a straw manufactory to help local workers when wartime deepened their poverty.

Menswear was virile, with martial overtones. Boots and riding coat were the gentleman's choice, with breeches adding an aristocratic touch or, perhaps, trend-setting skin-tight pantaloons. Men's shirts were made at home, by mothers, wives or sisters like Jane and Cassandra. In 1800 Jane was sending brother Charles shirts 'by the half-dozens as they are finished'. Tying the linen neckcloth became an art in itself. Older men, like Mr Austen, clung to powdered hair, while younger men like Francis and Charles wore their hair natural and cut short.

The Road to Town

Travel was by public coach, private carriage or horseback. Jane experienced all three, and showed some knowledge of carriage styles and driving. Her wealthy families reveal their status by the type of carriage and horses they can afford. Edward Austen could spend 60 guineas on a pair of carriage horses; the Austens managed to keep a carriage for just one year, in 1797. Travel by public coach meant eating at roadside inns. On one journey made with her parents, Jane discovered the loss of her boxes, with money, letters and papers, at an overnight stop. The landlord feared they had been put on the wrong coach, bound for Gravesend and the West Indies, so a messenger was sent in pursuit and the luggage retrieved. Mail also came by coach. The young Austens enjoyed being sent to collect letters from the Deane Gate Inn.

Jane's travels took her to several cities, two of which became her home. In 1801 Mr Austen decided to retire from Steventon, sell up, and take his wife and daughters to Bath. On hearing the news, Jane reportedly fainted. She had stayed in Bath before and used the city as the setting for *Northanger Abbey* (initially called *Susan*). Bath had libraries, Assembly Rooms, a theatre and firework displays, but Jane did not relish it as home. At Bath her writing tailed away.

The family lived at 4 Sydney Place, near Sydney Gardens, but she and Cassandra spent

ABOVE *Taking the waters at the Pump Room, Bath, in 1784. This Humphry Repton watercolour shows a scene that Jane knew well but may not have cared for. Bath attracted the sick, the hypochondriac, the gossip, the idler and many a rascal, too.*

LEFT *Sydney Gardens, Bath, an 1805 aquatint after John Claude Nattes (c. 1765–1822).*

ABOVE *Road journeys often meant spending hours or even days in a jolting vehicle, such as this stagecoach shown leaving Southampton.*

RIGHT *Jane and Cassandra trotted around the Hampshire country lanes in this donkey carriage, which now rests at the Jane Austen's House Museum in Chawton.*

more time away with friends and relations. In 1802, while with the Biggs of Manydown, Jane received a marriage proposal from Harris Bigg, which she accepted. Overnight she experienced a change of heart, however, and in the morning the sisters quickly left. Perhaps Jane remembered an earlier occasion at Manydown in 1796 when she had flirted enthusiastically with a visiting young Irishman named Tom Lefroy. The mutual attraction was noticed and he had been tactfully sent away, to save the two young people, too poor to marry, from an imprudent match.

In 1805 Jane's much-loved father died, soon after her friend Mrs Lefroy had been killed in a fall from a bolting horse. The Austen ladies changed lodgings for the third time since arriving in Bath and then, at Frank's suggestion, moved with him to Castle Square in Southampton, where the house had a garden for Jane to enjoy. Finally, in 1809,

Edward offered his mother and sisters the use of Chawton Cottage, near their old home in the Hampshire countryside.

A countrywoman at heart, Jane nevertheless enjoyed her visits to London, where her banker brother Henry lived with Eliza, and where in spring 1811 she corrected proofs at their home in Sloane Street. Jane was taken on a social whirl of theatres, exhibitions, galleries and great houses, but in 1813 Eliza died. Henry moved to Henrietta Street and, while on a visit in 1815, Jane met the Prince Regent's librarian at Carlton House. She was told His Royal Highness would find the dedication of her new novel acceptable. It was *Emma*. In 1816 Henry's bank failed, he was declared bankrupt and Jane's visits to London came to an end. A city dealer no more, Henry took the curacy at Chawton, settling down to the life of a country parson.

The Navy

Two of Jane Austen's brothers served in Nelson's navy. Francis, known first as Fly and later Frank, entered the Naval Academy at Portsmouth in 1786, just before his twelfth birthday, to be followed five years later by his brother Charles. Boy sailors usually joined a ship straight away as 'captain's servant', taking their uniform, a sea chest and £30–£40 a year allowance. Their father wanted the young Austens first to learn astronomy, mathematics and chronology, as well as French, dancing and handwriting, for diplomatic use. They were following a career traditional among younger sons of the clergy. Nelson was himself a son of the Church.

'With ships and sailors she felt herself at home,' wrote Jane's biographer, James Edward Leigh-Austen in 1870, and Britain's navy features strongly in both *Mansfield Park* and *Persuasion*. Indeed, *Persuasion*, written after Napoleon's capture and exile to Elba, was begun with the intent of raising naval morale after a loss of prestige in the American War of 1812. Jane was familiar with the highs and lows of naval life, the waits for promotion, years spent away from home, the uncertainty and danger. She wrote diligently every three or four weeks to her absent brothers, with news from home, but letters could take months to arrive.

The navy in Jane's novels represents order, efficiency and bravery, although one or two bad apples are allowed, among them Admiral Crawford. Fanny Price's Portsmouth home is presented, by way of contrast, as

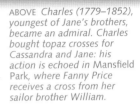

ABOVE *Charles (1779–1852), youngest of Jane's brothers, became an admiral. Charles bought topaz crosses for Cassandra and Jane: his action is echoed in* Mansfield Park, *where Fanny Price receives a cross from her sailor brother William.*

LEFT *The harbour at Portsmouth, about 1770. Jane knew the naval town well, both for its busy port and ships, and its more humdrum domestic side, as experienced by Fanny Price in* Mansfield Park.

ABOVE Men-O'-War and Small Craft at Portsmouth Harbour, *a painting by Thomas Whitcombe (1760–1824).*

RIGHT *Francis Austen (1774–1865), known as Frank, became Admiral of the Fleet and earned a knighthood.*

inefficient and grimy, and her parents slatternly. The Portsmouth where her brothers studied was a sailors' town, rife with drunkenness, prostitution and press gangs. The officers of the Austen drawing rooms, however, are successful, sensible, honourable and tender-hearted.

Navy life was dangerous. Of 100,000 seamen estimated killed in the wars of 1793–1815, just 7 per cent died in action. Disease and accident accounted for 80 per cent, while 13 per cent of deaths resulted from natural disasters or 'dangers of the sea', including fire and yellow jack (a fever contracted from mosquitoes). The Austen brothers survived, commanding crews that included criminals and press-ganged men. Francis, a strict captain, served under Nelson, who rated him 'an excellent young man', but he missed Trafalgar, to his great disappointment.

The brothers patrolled the North Sea, blockaded the French fleet in the Channel ports, were stationed in the Mediterranean off Spain, carried troops, escorted convoys to the Baltic, West Indies, India and China, and patrolled the North American station from Halifax to Bermuda. Charles was popular and kind-hearted. He served with the Cornish coastguard to deter smugglers of gin, brandy, silk, rum and tea, but was also ordered to suppress piracy in the Greek islands, where he lost his ship in a hurricane. He helped crush the slave trade and ended his career as a rear-admiral, leading the capture of Rangoon in Burma. At 73, he headed an expedition up the Irrawaddy River, where he died of cholera.

Francis also dealt with the Chinese, escorting a convoy to the Canton River in the teeth of marauding pirates on the mainland. He was commander of the North American and West Indian station in the Caribbean, operating against slave traders and exercising gunboat diplomacy off Venezuela and Nicaragua. He died aged 91 as Admiral of the Fleet.

The Army

If the Royal Navy was the senior service, the army had a special interest, too, for the Austens. When war between England and France broke out in 1793, Henry Austen forsook his studies at Oxford to join the militia, being stationed first at Southampton and then at Brighton, Ipswich, Chelmsford and Dublin among other towns. He also managed to take his degree.

The invasion threat meant that soldiers were a familiar sight, either on the march or encamped along the south coast. Basingstoke in 1794 was swelled with militia officers, adding interest to social prospects and partners for the Assembly balls. The army was also on the alert for any radical unrest in England. Food rioters around Newhaven in 1795 included men from Henry's regiment, and their punishment was severe: execution by firing squad before the entire Brighton garrison. Henry eventually became a captain and paymaster, which led him to his next career of banking.

RIGHT *Henry, fourth of the Austen brothers, left Oxford to join the militia and spent some time as an army officer. Of great charm, much-loved and forgiven, he progressed through the militia, banking and, when that failed, the Church. 'Oh! What a Henry!' was his sister's fond comment.*

Distrust of a standing army since the 17th-century Civil War meant that home defence in Britain was left mainly to volunteers and conscripts in local county militias. If volunteers were too few, a 'levy ballot' of men aged between 18 and 30 was required. Excluded from duty were peers, clergy, university residents, parish schoolmasters, apprentices, sailors and 'any poor man with more than one lawful child' (two

BELOW *Camped at Brighton: this 1803 painting by A.E. Eglinton shows the 10th Regiment of Dragoons. Soldiers in south-country towns aroused anxiety and excitement, among both local traders and young girls like those in Pride and Prejudice who so admired a man in regimentals.*

LEFT *The 52nd Regiment of Foot (Oxfordshire Light Infantry) fought with distinction in the Peninsular War and at Waterloo in 1815. Here its men are pictured in Portugal in 1810.*

BELOW *The victor of Waterloo: Arthur Wellesley, Duke of Wellington (1769–1852), a painting by Sir Thomas Lawrence (1769–1830).*

children in Scotland). The militia regiments formed a reserve of youngish, mostly fit men, able to fire a gun if only at game. Officers had to be land-owning gentlemen – not necessarily a guarantee of military competence.

Such officers arrive on the scene in *Pride and Prejudice*, much to Mrs Bennet's delight, and include the attractive Wickham, whose charm was as captivating as Henry Austen's seems to have been. Kitty and Lydia Bennet are 'well supplied with news and happiness' by the arrival of soldiers in Meryton for the winter, and they were no doubt also welcomed by local shopkeepers and tavern-owners. The officers in Meryton are generally a 'very creditable gentlemanlike set', though Mr Wickham, splendid in his regimentals, is revealed as being more show than substance. Wickham tells Elizabeth Bennet that 'a military life is not what I was intended for', the Church having been his intended profession. This may be another echo of brother Henry.

Although the army had not distinguished itself in the American wars, its reputation was restored in the Peninsular campaigns under the leadership of Sir John Moore and the Duke of Wellington. Despite those victories, the terrifying image of its low soldiery – ill-educated, brutally disciplined, badly fed and most dangerous when drunk – lingered on.

29

The Writer

Sense and Sensibility was Jane Austen's first published novel, appearing in 1811 as written 'By a Lady'. In 1813 came *Pride and Prejudice*, an immediate success which had taken the 20-year-old Jane a year to write in 1796. All the Austens were well-educated, read books of all kinds, and were writers of sermons, letters, verses, plays and logbooks. They listened, encouraged and entertained each other by committing words to paper. Jane's books were first read aloud to her family, but she clearly wrote also for her own amusement, beginning when a child with her *Juvenilia* – sketches, stories, plays and a history of England. She was following family tradition.

In 1790 she wrote *Love and Freindship* and in 1794 *Lady Susan*. Over the next four years at Steventon came three major novels: *Elinor and Marianne* (*Sense and Sensibility*), *First Impressions* (*Pride and Prejudice*) and *Susan* (*Northanger Abbey*). Jane's father, the scholar, appreciated his daughter's worth and wrote to enquire about

RIGHT *A modest advertisement in London's* Morning Chronicle *of Thursday, 31 October 1811. Amongst the notices for naval tenders, pharmacists and rooms to let is the announcement of a new novel,* Sense and Sensibility.

RIGHT *A painting of Chawton House and church in 1809, the year that Jane Austen settled in the village with her mother and sister. The move, made possible by brother Edward, proved a happy one.*

BELOW *Jane Austen spent much of her time in the drawing room at Chawton. The house is now a museum.*

ABOVE LEFT *The house in College Street, Winchester, where Jane Austen spent the last few weeks of her life and died in 1817.*

ABOVE RIGHT Winchester Cathedral, *watercolour of 1801 by John Buckler (1770–1851). Jane Austen is buried here. Cassandra watched her beloved sister's interment from the door, since women customarily did not stand at the graveside for the final part of the funeral.*

publication of *First Impressions*, but the publisher, Cadell, did not wish to read it. *Susan* fared better. With Henry's help it was sold in 1803 for £10, but was not published.

Jane and Cassandra, closely devoted, shared a well-tuned mutual understanding. They also shared their daily lives, duties, secrets, entertainment and work (much like Jane and Elizabeth Bennet in *Pride and Prejudice*). At Chawton, Cassandra undertook most of the domestic responsibilities to allow her sister to write. 'Composition seems to me impossible, with a head full of Joints of Mutton and doses of rhubarb.' Once Jane had risen, completed her piano practice and made breakfast, she could turn to her pen. Breakfast of toast or muffins, honey, rolls and butter, was taken with tea, of which Jane was particularly fond, and eaten by the fire at 9 a.m. This was Jane's only domestic task, apart from keeping the key of the wine and tea cupboard. A maid set the fire and filled the kettle.

Jane wrote in pen and ink on a small table as if she were writing a letter, ready to put down her pen and hide her paper away if she heard anyone coming. Ideas ran in her head all the time. Sometimes, when otherwise busy, she might jump up and rush to make a note as an idea struck her. At Chawton, after revising *Sense and Sensibility* and *Pride and Prejudice*, she wrote three more novels: *Mansfield Park*, *Emma* and *Persuasion*, the last while she was already ill so that it was published after her death.

Jane savoured her success. At last she had some money of her own ('Single women have a dreadful propensity for being poor') and she enjoyed seeking out portraits of her characters in London galleries. Her material came from people. She had a satirist's eye for hypocrisy and her aim was true. The caricaturists Hogarth and Rowlandson exposed folly and vice in high places; Jane Austen looked with wry humour at her own circle, relishing the contrariness of human nature. She was good with children and could have married, but chose instead the creativity of her imagination.

In 1817 she moved with Cassandra to Winchester for medical care and there died in her sister's arms. She was buried in Winchester Cathedral.

Places to Visit

Alton was the nearest town to Jane's home at Chawton. The Curtis Museum has a Jane Austen trail (High Street, Alton, Hampshire GU34 1BA; 0845 6035635; http://www3.hants. gov.uk/curtis-museum).

Basingstoke, Hampshire: Jane shopped here and danced at the Assembly Rooms above the town hall. Jane and Cassandra visited the home of the Chute family at The Vyne, to play cards and for dances (Vyne Road, Sherborne St John, Basingstoke, Hampshire RG24 9HL; 01256 883858; www.nationaltrust. org.uk/main/w-thevyne).

Bath: the watering place for the fashionable of Jane Austen's day, and where she lived from 1801 to 1806. The Jane Austen Centre and Regency Tearoom is at 40 Gay Street, Queen Square, Bath BA1 2NT; 01225 443000; www.janeausten.co.uk.

Brighton: the resort of the fashionable in Regency England, though disliked by Jane Austen. The Royal Pavilion was completed shortly after she died (4-5 Pavilion Buildings, Brighton BN1 1EE; 03000 290900; www.brighton-hove-rpml.org.uk/Pages/home.aspx).

Canterbury: Jane visited the cathedral (CT1 2EH; 01227 762862; www.canterbury-cathedral.org/), and the town to see Mrs Knight and friends in The Close and cathedral precincts.

Chatsworth House, the grand Peak District home of the Dukes of Devonshire, has a first edition of *Pride and Prejudice* among its many treasures (Bakewell, Derbyshire DE45 1PP; 01246 565300; www.chatsworth.org/).

Chawton, where Jane spent the last years of her life and where she worked on her major novels. Visit Jane Austen's House Museum (Chawton, Alton, Hampshire GU34 1SD; 01420 83262; www.jane-austens-house-museum.org.uk/), the Chawton House library and Church of St Nicholas.

Chilham Castle, Kent, where Jane went to a ball in 1801 (Chilham, Canterbury, Kent CT4 8DB; www.chilham-castle.co.uk/).

Deane Gate Inn was where the children collected the post and may have been used for stabling the family's horses (Deane, Basingstoke RG25 3AX; 01256 780226; http://www.britishpubguide.com/cgi-bin/pubsearch. cgi?results:Hampshire:100775).

Godmersham estate was visited by Jane to see her brother Edward, who inherited it (http://www.kentdowns.org. uk/40places/19.%20Godmersham%20Park.html).

Goodnestone Park (Canterbury, Kent CT3 1PL; 01304 840107; http://www.goodnestoneparkgardens. co.uk/): Jane visited here in 1796 and began writing *Pride and Prejudice* soon after.

ABOVE *Jane Austen's little writing table in the parlour at her house at Chawton.*

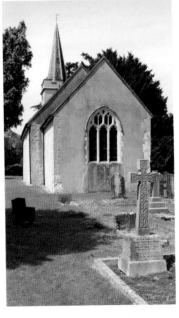

LEFT *A view from the churchyard of St Nicholas's, Steventon, which Jane Austen was so reluctant to leave.*